A Pocket Full of Rhyme

Daddy and me...

By
Janice Williams

Grosvenor House
Publishing Limited

This book is published by
Grosvenor House Publishing Ltd
Link House
140 The Broadway, Tolworth, Surrey, KT6 7HT.
www.grosvenorhousepublishing.co.uk

A CIP record for this book
is available from the British Library

ISBN 978-1-83975-517-0

This book is in memory of Tom, our beautiful son, loving brother to Tim, devoted daddy to Daisy and soul mate to Amy.

The sun won't shine quite as bright,
Since daddy went away.
He took his drums to the angels
To teach them how to play.
So, when I'm feeling tearful,
And sometimes oh so glum,
I look towards the rainbow,
Where daddy plays his drum.

Daddy and me, we used to be,
The best at scrubbing our teeth.
We would scrub at the bottom
And scrub at the top,
And scrub all the bits underneath.

Daddy would say, "Daisy, this way"
Open your mouth really wide.
We would scrub at the bottom and scrub at the top,
And my mouth would feel minty inside.

We're having a party, with lots of balloons,
Jelly and ice cream too.
We'll play lots of games, shouting out names,
So everyone knows what to do.
The magician is here to show us his tricks,
Can turn a dog into a cat!
Just can't believe, the things up his sleeve
As rabbits jump out of his hat!
Then comes the cake, with candles atop,
The biggest I ever did see!
And everyone stands, clapping their hands
As they sing happy birthday to me.

Daisy and I, gazed up at the sky,
And Daisy started to frown,
I know, that it's true, the sky's always blue,
What would happen if it turned brown?
Said I in deep ponder, I never gave wonder,
I guess it always shall rain,
There'll be mud on the floor and all round the door,
And we'll never play outside again.
Daisy then said, as she cocked her sweet head,
"Nanny, how come you're always so clever?"
Then Daisy and me, went in for our tea,
And the sky stayed as blue as ever.

I know a far-off wonderland,
Across a misty mountain.
There's birds and bees and chocolate trees
And a coca cola fountain.
Unicorns and dragons too,
And cotton candy ditches,
Magic spells and wishing wells,
And castles for the witches.
Enchanted woods where fairies dwell,
And knights in fancy dress
Bravely fight with all their might,
For damsels in distress.
It's an easy place to get to,
All you do is look.
Wonderland is close at hand
Between the pages of a book.

Daddy liked to bake me cakes,
He'd let me help him too.
Mixing up ingredients,
There's always lots to do.
We would always sing when baking,
As daddy liked a tune,
But best of all, just at the end
We both would lick the spoon.

We're going on a picnic,
For our Sunday treat,
The sun is shining brightly
And there's lots of things to eat.
Nanny has been baking,
Can't count the things she's made
But there's lots of tuna sandwiches
And homemade lemonade.
We'll sit by daddy's garden,
So, his smile is with us too,
And Uncle Tim will chase me
As I try to run from view.
Then we'll all sit down together,
Our troubles, far away.
Oh, I wish it could be picnic time,
Every single day!

All day it has rained,
A steady downpour,
Bouncing off the ground
Like it's never rained before.
Splashing off the windows,
Puddles deep and grey,
Watching from the bedroom,
I can't go out to play.
The rain can be so dreary,
Damp and boring too.
So, I think about my daddy,
And wonder, what he'd do.

Daddy bought a special seat
To put upon his bike.
Far and wide we both would ride
To places that I like.

We would cycle to the big green park,
Then back in time for tea.
I'd see the trees and feel the breeze
With daddy, bike and me.

In daddy's ever after land,
Rainbows grab you by the hand.
Dreams come true for there are many
And wishes sell for two a penny.
Fluffy clouds float high above,
And everyone is full of love.
Angels all around you stand
In daddy's ever after land.

I found a secret swing,
Hanging from a tree.
So, I made a secret wish,
Only known to me...
(and daddy)

Stars are twinkling overhead,
Time for us to go to bed.
Make a wish, it may come true,
One for me, and one for you

I wrote and illustrated a Pocket Full of Rhyme, Daddy and Me... in memory of my son Thomas and daddy to my four-year-old granddaughter, Daisy.

The illustrations are taken from the many beautiful and happy photographs of Thomas and Daisy together, which Daisy loves to look at.

Thomas played the drums for Hot Tramp, a local band that was very popular, followed by many.

His epilepsy never hindered him from achieving what he wanted to do and his greatest achievement in his life is Daisy.

I hope that this book can help ease the sorrow of a child losing a parent.

Daddy and me

Lightning Source UK Ltd.
Milton Keynes UK
UKHW050657120421
381840UK00005B/79